Fife Council Education Department
King's Road Primary School
King's Crescent, Rosyth KY11 2RS

Food
POTATOES

Louise Spilsbury

www.heinemann.co.uk/library
Visit our website to find out more information about Heinemann Library books.

To order:
☎ Phone 44 (0) 1865 888066
▤ Send a fax to 44 (0) 1865 314091
▢ Visit the Heinemann Bookshop at www.heinemann.co.uk/library to browse our catalogue and order online.

First published in Great Britain by Heinemann Library,
Halley Court, Jordan Hill, Oxford OX2 8EJ
a division of Reed Educational and Professional Publishing Ltd.
Heinemann is a registered trademark of Reed Educational & Professional Publishing Ltd.

OXFORD MELBOURNE AUCKLAND
JOHANNESBURG BLANTYRE GABORONE
IBADAN PORTSMOUTH (NH) USA CHICAGO

Designed by Celia Floyd
Originated by Ambassador Litho Ltd
Printed by South China Printing Co in Hong Kong

ISBN 0 431 12707 7
05 04 03 02 01
10 9 8 7 6 5 4 3 2 1

British Library Cataloguing in Publication Data
Spilsbury, Louise
  Potatoes. – (Food)
  1. Potatoes 2. Cookery (Potatoes)
  I. Title
  641.3'521

Acknowledgements
The Publishers would like to thank the following for permission to reproduce photographs:
AKG p.9; Anthony Blake /J Lee p.4; Gareth Boden pp.7, 22, 23, 25, 28, 29; Ardea /Chris Knights p.17, /John Mason p.16; Bruce Coleman Collection/Dr Eckart Pott p.13; Corbis /Jeffry W Myers p.24, /Ted Spiegel p.6, /Michael S Yamashita p.21; FLPA /J C Allen p.11, /Peter Dean p.15, /N J Thomas p.14; Holt Studios/Nigel Cattlin pp.18, 19; Oxford Scientific Films /Breck P Kent p.5, / Colin Monteath p.10, /Harry Taylor p.12; Tony Stone Images p.20; Werner Forman Archive p.8..

Cover photograph reproduced with permission of Gareth Boden.

Every effort has been made to contact copyright holders of any material reproduced in this book. Any omissions will be rectified in subsequent printings if notice is given to the Publisher.

CONTENTS

Words written in bold, **like this**, are explained in the Glossary.

WHAT ARE POTATOES?

Potatoes are **vegetables**. They are an important food for many people. Across the world people eat more potatoes than any other vegetable.

Potatoes grow from potato plants, but you cannot see the potatoes growing. They are a part of the plant that grows under the ground.

KINDS OF POTATOES

There are over 100 different kinds of potatoes. They look and taste quite different, but all potatoes contain **starch** and water.

Waxy potatoes have a lot of water and not much starch. They keep their shape when you cook them. Floury potatoes have lots of starch and little water. They are fluffy when cooked.

waxy potato   floury potato

IN THE PAST

Potatoes were grown in South America more than 6000 years ago. This picture shows people from **Peru** picking potatoes. It is over 400 years old.

Spanish **explorers** went to South America over 500 years ago. They brought potatoes back to Europe. Later, potatoes became popular in North America and Australia, too.

AROUND THE WORLD

As long as it does not get too cold at night, potatoes can grow almost anywhere. They can grow in cool, damp places like this farm in Nepal, in **Asia**.

Potatoes can also grow in hot, dry places. This huge farm is in America. It grows thousands of tonnes of potatoes to sell each year.

LOOKING AT POTATOES

Potato plants grow from **seed potatoes**. When these are planted in the ground, they grow **roots** down into the soil. Then, **shoots** grow up towards the light.

new shoots

seed potato

In spring, potato plants grow leaves and flowers in the sunlight. The leaves make food for the new potatoes that are growing on the roots underground.

PLANTING POTATOES

On this potato farm, the farmer uses a tractor to pull a **plough**. The plough breaks up the soil. When the soil is ready, the farmer plants the **seed potatoes**.

A machine called a planter puts the seed potatoes in the soil. It drops lots of seed potatoes into the ground in a short time.

GROWING POTATOES

Potato plants, like all plants, need sunlight and water to grow. If the weather is very dry, farmers use special machines to spray water on the potato plants.

While the potato plants are growing, they need to be protected from **pests** and **diseases**. Some farmers spray the plants to stop them being damaged.

Colorado beetle

LIFTING POTATOES

When the potatoes are ready, farmers kill the leaves of the plants with a special spray. This makes the **skins** of the potatoes under the ground become thicker.

A machine called a harvester lifts the potatoes out of the ground. This machine also separates the potatoes from the soil.

POTATOES TO US

After the farmers dig up the potatoes, they check them. They look at the potatoes and throw away any bad or **rotten** ones.

Some potatoes are sold straight away, others are stored to be sold later. Farmers put them into special rooms to keep them fresh. These rooms are cool and dark.

EATING POTATOES

People cook potatoes before they eat them. Potatoes are cooked and eaten in many ways. They can be boiled, steamed, roasted, baked or fried.

mashed

boiled

baked

Potatoes are also **processed** to make lots of different **products** such as chips, hash browns and crisps. Potatoes are sold **frozen** and in cans, and also as **dried** mashed potato.

GOOD FOR YOU

Potatoes are a **carbohydrate**. This means they are a kind of food that gives us **energy**. We use up energy in everything we do.

Potatoes also contain **vitamins** and **fibre**. Vitamins are **nutrients** that help our bodies grow and protect us from illness. Fibre helps our bodies to stay healthy.

25

HEALTHY EATING

You need to eat different kinds of food to keep well. This food pyramid shows you how much of each different food you need.

Potatoes are in the group of **vegetables** in the middle of the pyramid. You need to eat some of the things in that group every day.

You should eat some of the foods shown at the bottom of the pyramid every day, too. You need only tiny amounts of the foods at the top.

The food in each part of the pyramid helps your body in different ways.

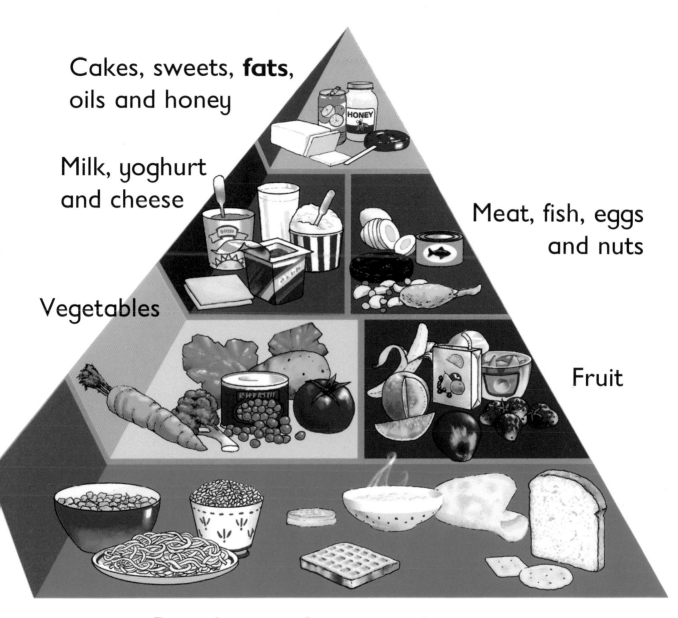

Cakes, sweets, **fats**, oils and honey

Milk, yoghurt and cheese

Meat, fish, eggs and nuts

Vegetables

Fruit

Bread, **cereals**, rice and pasta

BAKED POTATO RECIPE

1 Take the potatoes and wash the skins well.

2 Prick each potato with a fork.

You will need:
- 1 big potato for each person
- butter
- grated cheese

Ask an adult to help you!

28

3 Bake the potatoes in a hot oven (200°C/360°F/Gas mark 6) for about an hour.

4 Cut them open and put a little butter and some grated cheese in each potato.

GLOSSARY

Asia   part of the world made up of different countries, including China, Japan, Thailand and India. Asian means people or things from Asia.

carbohydrate   kind of food that gives us energy

cereals   grains like wheat and rice that are used to make foods like flour, bread and breakfast cereals

disease   diseases can harm plants and animals

dried   some foods are dried before being packed and sold. They can be kept for a long time before people use them.

energy   all living things need energy to live, move and grow. We get energy from our food.

explorers   people who travel to new places. In the past, explorers set out to find new lands, food or gold.

fat   type of food. Butter, oil and margarine are kinds of fat. It is not healthy to eat or drink too many fatty foods.

fibre   part of a fruit, vegetable or cereal that helps keep our bodies healthy

frozen   when food is kept as cold as ice in order to keep it fresh

nutrients goodness in food that we need to stay healthy

Peru country in South America, which includes parts of the Andes Mountains

pests insects or other animals which eat plants and damage them

plough machine that breaks up the soil to make it ready for planting seeds

processed treated to make into something else. Potatoes are processed to make crisps.

product something that is made to be sold

roots plant parts that grow down into the ground. They take in water and nutrients from the soil.

rotten going bad, not fit to eat

seed potatoes small potatoes with shoots that will grow into potato plants when planted

shoot first stem and leaves of a new plant

skin outer layer of a vegetable such as a potato

starch kind of carbohydrate

vegetables parts of plants that we can eat. Vegetables include carrots, potatoes, and lettuce.

vitamins group of nutrients that keep your body healthy and help you grow

MORE BOOKS TO READ

Plants: How plants grow, Angela Royston, Heinemann Library, 1999

Senses: Tasting, K. Hartley, C. Macro, P. Taylor, Heinemann Library, 2000

Body Wise: Why Do I feel Hungry? Sharon Cromwell, Heinemann Library

What's For Lunch? Potatoes, Franklin Watts

Potato: A Tale From the Great Depression, National Geographic Society

INDEX

32

Titles in the *Food* series include:

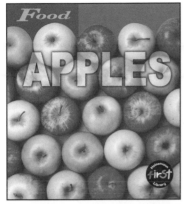

Hardback   0 431 12708 5

Hardback   0 431 12700 X

Hardback   0 431 12702 6

Hardback   0 431 12706 9

Hardback   0 431 12701 8

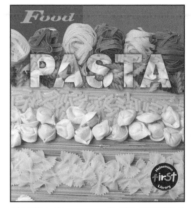

Hardback   0 431 12703 4

Hardback   0 431 12707 7

Hardback   0 431 12705 0

Find out about the other titles in this series on our website www.heinemann.co.uk/library